P9-BYV-762

SCHOLASTIC
News
Nonfiction Readers

A Shark Pup Grows Up

by
Pam Zollman

Children's Press®
A Division of Scholastic Inc.
New York Toronto London Auckland Sydney
Mexico City New Delhi Hong Kong
Danbury, Connecticut

These content vocabulary word builders
are for grades 1-2.

Consultant: William Fink
Professor of Ecology and Evolutionary Biology
University of Michigan
Ann Arbor, Michigan

Curriculum Specialist: Linda Bullock

Special thanks to the Kansas City Zoo

Photo Credits:

Photographs © 2005: Corbis Images/Jeffrey L. Rotman: back cover; Dembinsky Photo Assoc.: 2, 15 (Jesse Cancelmo), 23 top left (E. R. Degginger); marinethemes.com/Kelvin Aitken: front cover, 1, 20 bottom, 20 top, 21; Nature Picture Library Ltd.: 5, 10 (Jurgen Freund), 23 bottom left (Constantinos Petrinos); Photo Researchers, NY/Mark Harmel: 23 top right; Seapics.com: 4 bottom left, 16 (Phillip Colla), 5 bottom left, 11 (Mark Conlin), 4 top right, 19 bottom (David B. Fleetham), 5 top left, 8 (Howard Hall), 4 bottom right, 5 bottom right, 7, 9, 13, 20 center left, 23 bottom right (Doug Perrine), 17 (Masa Ushioda), 19 top (James D. Watt).

Book Design: Simonsays Design!

Library of Congress Cataloging-in-Publication Data

Zollman, Pam.
    A shark pup grows up / by Pam Zollman.
        p. cm. — (Scholastic news nonfiction readers)
    Includes bibliographical references and index.
    ISBN 0-516-24945-2 (lib. bdg.)
    1. Sharks—Development—Juvenile literature. I. Title. II. Series.
    QL638.9.Z65 2005
    597.3'139—dc22
                        2005003292

1 2 3 4 5 6 7 8 9 10 R 14 13 12 11 10 09 08 07 06 05

CONTENTS

WORD HUNT

Look for these words as you read. They will be in **bold**.

adult
(**ah**-duhlt)

fish
(fish)

gill slit
(gil slit)

4

egg case
(eg kays)

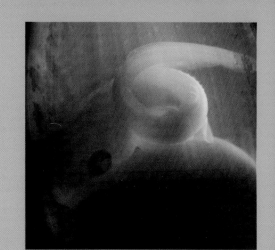

embryo
(**em**-bree-oh)

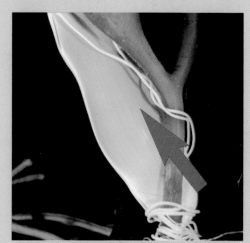

hatch
(hach)

pouch
(pouch)

5

Shark Pups!

What is a shark pup?

A shark pup is a baby shark.

Sharks are **fish**. Fish live in water. They have fins and gills.

The **gill slits** are openings to the gills.

gill slit

fins

Sharks breathe through gills.
The gills are under the gill slits.

Do you know how a shark pup is born?

Some sharks **hatch** from eggs. Hard cases cover the eggs.

Some **egg cases** look like **pouches** or bags.

Some egg cases look like screws.

egg case

pouch

9

A shark **embryo** grows inside each egg case.

How does the pup hatch?

The pup uses its sharp teeth to break open the egg case.

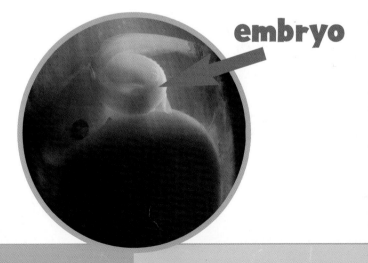

embryo

Look! This shark pup is coming out of its egg case.

Most shark pups do not hatch from eggs.

They grow inside their mother.

A shark pup can swim when it is born.

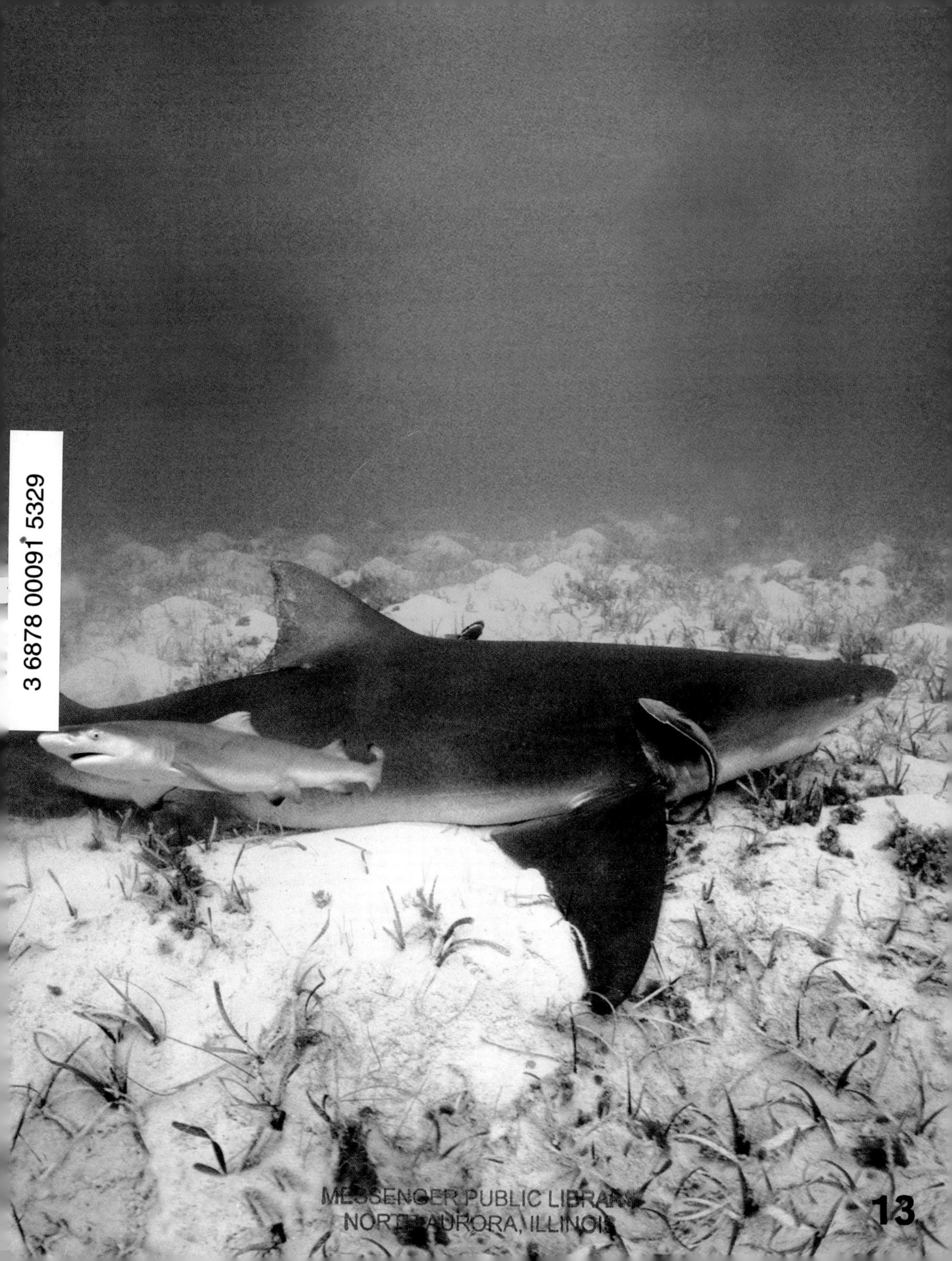

Watch out, pups!

Bigger sharks might eat you.

Pups swim fast to get away.

Their tails push them through the water.

This shark may be looking for food. Watch out, pups!

Do you know what hungry pups eat?

Pups eat crabs and fish.

They eat clams and squid, too.

fish

This shark pup may eat some of these fish.

There are many kinds of shark pups.

They grow up to be **adult** sharks.

Then they can have pups of their own.

This is an adult
Whale shark.

This is an adult
Great White shark.

19

A Shark Pup Grows Up!

1····

This mother shark lays an egg case.

2·····

This is the egg case. It looks like a screw.

3·····

Look! The shark pup is coming out of the egg case.

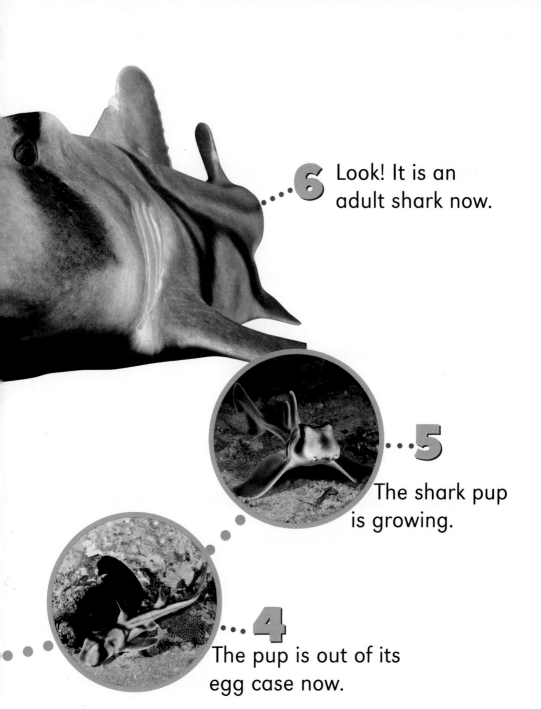

6 Look! It is an adult shark now.

5 The shark pup is growing.

4 The pup is out of its egg case now.

YOUR NEW WORDS

adult (**ah**-duhlt) a person or animal that is grown-up

egg case (eg kays) a layer around an egg that keeps it safe

embryo (**em**-bree-oh) a baby that is growing inside of an egg case or in its mother

fish (fish) an animal that lives in water and has fins, and gills

gill slit (gil slit) gill slits cover a fish's gills

hatch (hach) to break out of an egg

pouch (pouch) a bag

WHAT ELSE LIVES IN THE OCEAN?

A clam!

A jellyfish!

A sea horse!

A squid!

INDEX

FIND OUT MORE

Book:
Eyewitness: Shark
by Miranda MacQuitty (DK Publishing, 2004)

Website:
http://www.enchantedlearning.com/subjects/sharks/

MEET THE AUTHOR:

Pam Zollman is the award-winning author of short stories, articles, and books for kids. She is the author of *North Dakota* (Scholastic/Children's Press) and the other Life Cycle books in this series. She lives in Pennsylvania where there are no sharks.